About this book

Did you know that many of our sports are thousands of years old? The Olympic Games, for instance, were started by the ancient Greeks, and the Romans raced their chariots to thrill the crowds in a sport which was just as dangerous as motor racing today.

This new *Eyewitness* book tells the story of how the earliest sports began, and how many of them changed into the sports we know today. You can see pictures of the first wrestling and boxing matches, of gladiator fights, jousting and tournaments, fencing and judo. For hundreds of years men used animals in sports, often very cruelly. Happily, many of these bloodthirsty sports have been banned.

The sports that attract the biggest crowds today are football, rugby, horseracing and tennis. Do *you* have a favourite? If so, you will probably find a picture in this book that shows you how it all started.

Some of the words printed in *italics* may be new to you. You can look them up in the word list on page 92.

AN EYEWITNESS BOOK

Sport through the Ages

PETER WILSON

WAYLAND PUBLISHERS LONDON

More Eyewitness Books

Frontispiece: British runner Alan Simpson.

SBN 85340 335 X
Copyright © 1974 by Wayland Publishers Ltd
101 Grays Inn Road, London, WC1
Filmset by Keyspools Ltd, Golborne, Lancs
Printed by The Pitman Press, Bath, Somerset

Contents

1. Combat Sports

When you see a large crowd of boys and girls gathered in a circle on your school field or playground, you will probably be right if you guess there is a "fight" going on. See if you can think of some answers to these two questions: why do men fight, and why do people find watching a fight so interesting?

In the past every man needed to fight to stay alive. Cavemen had to protect their dwellings and their families from human enemies and dangerous beasts. When men began to live together in towns and cities or as nations, they formed armies to protect them from invaders. At this time combat sports had two good purposes. The first was for military practice. Soldiers needed to be fit and able to use their weapons. But what about the people who no longer had to fight every day to stay alive? They still had to keep fit and might need to fight in an emergency. They might even start fighting among themselves! How much better if they could fight without hurting themselves too much. This was the second good reason for combat sports.

This chapter will show you that many combat sports have been cruel and dangerous. People who did not want to get hurt could watch others and imagine themselves in the place of a wrestler, a gladiator or a boxer. Today, our boxers fight under strict rules to stop them from being too badly hurt. But the people in the crowd are not very different from the Roman mob. They are still satisfying their need to fight, but from the safety of their seats.

WRESTLING GREEK STYLE. Wrestling is the simplest of combat sports. The contestants have no weapons but the strength of their muscles. The Greeks loved it as a sport and as a way of training boys for warfare. All Greek boys learned to wrestle at school, and fought without clothing, their bodies covered in oil. Thucydides, the Greek historian, tells us "The Spartans were the first to display themselves naked in public, and rub themselves with oil for athletic contests." Athletes throughout Greece were quick to follow their example. Over three rounds, a wrestler tried to throw his opponent to the ground without falling himself. At the end of the contest the wrestlers had to scrape the mixture of oil and sand from their bodies, and rounded things off with a much-needed bath.

IRON "BOXING GLOVES." We might think that modern boxing is a very tough sport, but look at the way the Romans boxed! Their "boxing gloves," called *caesti*, were made of bull-hide straps studded with iron or lead pellets. They were obviously designed to do a lot of damage, unlike modern boxing gloves which are meant to protect. Roman boxers wore no protective clothing and were often severely wounded, which is just what the audience found entertaining. Horace, the Roman poet, tells us they would clamour for boxing during a play, if they found it boring. Most professional boxers were slaves or poor men hoping to buy freedom with their prize money. We know of one famous champion, called Horus, who became a philosopher on his retirement.

STADIUM OF CRUELTY. Looking at the empty ruins of a Roman *amphitheatre*, it is hard to believe that such great buildings were intended for the mass killing of men and animals. This one, called the Colosseum, was started by the Roman emperor Vespasian. It had four great terraces for spectators, each terrace reserved for a certain class of people. The lowest terrace or *podium* was for wealthy or powerful men and held the emperor's box. The highest terrace without seats was for very poor people and slaves. Where the floor of the arena is missing, you can see the underground chambers where wild beasts were kept.

UNEQUAL COMBAT. The *retiarius* was the only gladiator who could run away from the fight without being booed by the mob. He had to gain ground from the heavily-armed *secutor*, then turn and cast his net in the hope of trapping his opponent. If the throw was successful, the retiarius could move in with his trident and finish the fight. But more often the secutor pushed aside the net with his shield and the fight went on. The secutor chased his opponent, trying to smash the trident from his hands. If the retiarius lost his trident as well, he was done for and had to choose between fighting hand-to-hand or appealing for mercy.

APPEALING FOR MERCY. Gladiators faced the possibility of a brutal death whenever they entered the arena. Before the contest, as the Roman historian Suetonius tells us, they cried to the royal box: "Hail *Caesar*, we who are about to die salute you." One of the gladiators in this picture is helpless and raises his hand to beg for his life. If he has pleased the mob, there is a chance the emperor will turn up his thumb to grant him mercy. More often the mob will yell for his death and the emperor will turn his thumb down. At this sign the victor cuts his opponent's throat. Then an attendant, disguised as Death, strikes the victim's head with a hammer to make sure he is dead. The *libitinarii* remove the corpse on a stretcher.

NOVELTY FIGHTS.   Easily bored by the usual kinds of fight, the Roman mob demanded different methods of combat to break the monotony. There were *essedarii*, gladiators who fought from chariots. To add to the excitement, an organ played loud flourishes while the chariots twisted, turned and rammed each other on the sand. The gladiator depended on the skill of his driver to save them both from death or severe injury. Another novelty was the *naumachia* or sea battle. Some arenas could be flooded by underground reservoirs, and boats manned by criminals battered each other on these artificial lakes. Boarding-parties completed the slaughter and there were usually few survivors.

TOURNAMENTS.   One of the most highly organized combat sports of the Middle Ages was the tournament. Any number of knights and noblemen took part in a tournament, all charging at the same time. Before the contest began, the officer-at-arms, a sort of referee, made sure that all the contestants were "gentlemen of name and arms." Most weapons were blunted, for the tournament provided military practice, especially for young knights. Sometimes real weapons were used. At a tournament in Germany in 1249, sixty knights were killed, some being trampled to death or choking in the dust.

MEDIEVAL JOUSTS. Only two knights took part in a joust. They agreed on the kind of weapons to be used by touching shields, each shield representing a certain weapon. Before 1443, the jousts were more dangerous because the contestants rode straight at each other. A direct blow, even from a blunted lance, could cause serious injury. After 1443, a wooden barrier was placed between the jousters, who had to deal their blows at an angle, causing much less damage. Knights often fought in the name of a lady, and women decided the overall winner of a series of jousts as well as presenting the prizes. A day of jousting often ended with a banquet and dancing.

TILTING AT THE QUINTAIN.   Using a blunt lance against a wooden statue might seem harmless enough, but the results could be painful. Tilting at the *quintain* was good military practice for men of lower rank who could not take part in jousts and tournaments. The quintain was mounted on a pivot and a blow from the lance made it spin round. As Stow, the English writer, says, "He that hit not the broad end of the quintain was of all men laughed to scorn, and he that hit it full, if he rid not the faster, had a sound blow on his neck with a bag of sand on the other end." After the lance was no longer used in warfare, the quintain's entertainment value kept it popular, especially at wedding feasts.

SCHOOL FOR SWORDSMEN. In 1540 Henry VIII of England set up a company of fencers called "The Maisters of the Noble Science of Defence." Henry wanted to improve on the old sort of fencing with sword and buckler, a kind of shield. Sword and buckler contests were an excuse for fighting in the streets at holiday times. Henry's masters ran schools of fencing where there were four grades: scholars, free scholars, provosts and masters. To become a master a swordsman had to fight other masters with several different kinds of sword and dagger. The company broke up at the time of the *Commonwealth*, and fencing became a sort of prize-fighting where money, not "science," was all important.

BARE-KNUCKLE BOXING. This could only be the start of the fight! By the end of the contest both boxers would be covered in cuts and bruises and hardly able to stand. The first great prize-fighter was Jack Broughton, who in 1741 killed his opponent in the ring. Broughton swore never to fight again and drew up a set of rules for boxing. These rules made

fighting more popular as they banned the clubs and staffs earlier fighters had used when things were going badly for them. But tripping, kicking and strangling were still common ways of dealing with an opponent. Broughton also invented the first protective boxing gloves, called *mufflers*, but they were for training bouts only.

JAPANESE WRESTLING CIRCUS. Japanese people are usually short and light, but not their wrestlers. These giants eat and train in a special way to build up their size. Most of them are six feet tall and weigh over twenty stone, but they are still very quick on their feet. Sumo, as Japanese wrestling is called, is an ancient sport. The first match we know of was fought in 23 B.C., but there were probably many matches before that. The wrestlers fight in a ring of rush mats and fights are very short, sometimes lasting a few seconds. To win, a wrestler must force his opponent out of the ring, or make him touch the ground with any part of his body except his feet.

ENGLISH WRESTLING STYLES. The men of Devon and Cornwall had developed their own style of wrestling as far back as Saxon times. Over the years they made a set of rules for their wrestling, and proper methods of holding and throwing, like this one. The highest prize was a belt and the winner could wear this to church to show off his victory. They wore jackets by which they could pull and throw each other. The men of Cumberland and Westmorland were also great rivals at wrestling, but their rules were different from the Cornish ones and they did not wear jackets. From all over the Lake District, thousands of people flocked to Grasmere for the games, where local wrestlers fought for the championship.

FENCING DISPLAY. This Victorian display of fencing was put on as part of a "gymnastics meeting." At this time people were again taking an interest in fencing as a science, while bare-knuckle boxing provided more bloodthirsty entertainment. The *foils* were buttoned and the fencers now wore face masks, so it was not so dangerous a sport. As a result, schools and towns formed their own fencing clubs. These clubs set up the Amateur Fencing Association in 1898, and held their first fencing championships.

TAKING A COUNT. This has not happened very
often to Cassius Clay, now called Mohammed Ali.
Here, Henry Cooper, the English heavyweight fighter,
has managed to knock him down. Taking a count was
one of the rules drawn up by the Marquess of
Queensbury in 1865. He wanted to make boxing
safer and more attractive. His other rules provided for
padded gloves and three-minute rounds with a rest in
between, and he banned wrestling holds too. But
boxing is still a tough sport. Henry Cooper had to
retire from this fight, because his cut eyes were
pouring with blood.

ELECTRIC FOILS. Fencing is a much safer and faster sport now than it has ever been. The women in this picture are using electric equipment which makes a bell ring when there is a touch. Three different swords are used in Olympic competition: foil, epee and sabre. The foil and sabre both bend, but the epee is stiff, and each sword has different parts of the body for targets. But no-one gets hurt in modern fencing; protective clothing and face-masks see to that.

JUDO.   The art of falling without being hurt must be
learned in judo, for contestants often crash to the floor
after a throw. At the start of a bout the opponents bow
to each other in the style of the Japanese who invented
judo. Then they grip each other's jackets and belts,
trying to pull, push, trip and throw each other to the
ground. The colour of a judo belt shows how good a
person is at the sport. A beginner wears a white belt,
but an expert wears a black one. Judo has become one
of the most popular combat sports of recent times,
and was a part of the Olympic games for the first time
in 1964.

2. Animals and Sport

In the introduction to the first chapter, we saw that early man needed to fight to live. He also needed to hunt, for both food and clothing. Animals played two different parts in hunting. Some were the prey, and others, those animals man found he could train to help him, were his partners in the hunt. Dogs and horses were best at this. Even when he did not need to hunt for food, man found there was great pleasure in riding and hunting, so it became a sporting activity.

Horses were useful in battle too. Good cavalry and charioteers often helped to win the day. To practise their horsemanship, warriors held horse-races and chariot-races and these became part of the games in Greece and Rome.

It is much harder to understand or explain why men enjoyed animal-baiting. Thankfully, most baiting has died out, unless we think of Spanish bullfighting as a kind of bait. However, in real baiting man was completely safe and only the animals tore each other to pieces. But in bullfighting the *matador* risks his life whenever he steps into the ring.

Nowadays animals are usually man's partners in sport. Horse and rider work as a team on the race-course or in the jumping arena. And, there is little doubt which member of the team is better cared for!

BIG-GAME HUNTING. The Greeks had no powerful shooting weapons, so spears, axes and daggers
were used for hunting. This meant that the prey had
to be captured first. The Greeks had different kinds of
nets for catching animals, there was a fine one for
hares, and a large one made of thick rope for big-game.
Dogs chased the prey into the nets and the hunters
followed on horseback. The most famous Greek
ruler, Alexander the Great, conquered lands as far
away as India. Here his hunting parties could hunt the
big cats, like this panther, which did not live wild
in their native land.

GREEK CHARIOT RACING. The four-horse chariot race was the grandest event at the ancient Olympic Games. It was different from all the other events, because the owner of the horses and chariot hired professional drivers. We know that Alcibiades, a rich general, entered nine chariots at the Games in 416 B.C. and won first, second and fourth prizes. But long before the Olympic Games began, Greek warriors loved to chariot race. Homer, the Greek poet, tells us about a race that was part of the funeral games of the warrior Patroclus. In this race only two horses pulled each chariot. At the signal, the charioteers "all gave their horses the whip, shook the reins on their backs and set them going . . . they yelled at their horses who flew along in a cloud of dust."

DANGEROUS TURNING-POST.   In Roman chariot races crashes were most likely to happen at the *metae*, or turning-posts, like the one pictured above. The seven lap races were run in the Circus Maximus, an enormous stadium at least twice the size of the famous one at Wembley in London. The four chariots wore the colours of their *factions:* white, red, green and blue, and every spectator backed his

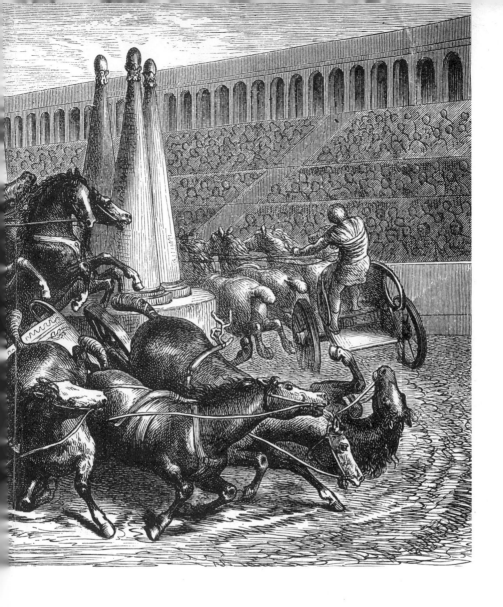

favourite faction as well as his favourite team of
horses. These horses were trained from the age of
three and had their first race at five years old. Some
horses won fame throughout the Roman Empire. One
Roman, called Pompeianus, decorated the floor of his
bathing-house with the words: "Win or lose, we love
you Polydoxus," in praise of his favourite horse.

BEAST AGAINST BEAST. Imagine the terror and rage of a lion chased from its cage by men with burning straw into an arena surrounded by roaring spectators. Facing it would be a tiger or a bull, also maddened by fire and whips. A deadly fight followed for the mob's amusement, and the winner, torn and wounded, was killed off by special beast-slaughterers. The Romans dragged every kind of known animal into the arena. The elephant and rhinoceros were favourites, as they were slow to anger but showed terrible fury when they were mad. The most revolting thing is the size of the slaughter. Suetonius tells us that five thousand animals were killed in one day for the opening ceremony of the Colosseum in 80 A.D.

MAN AGAINST BEAST.   Armed with a *venabulum*, the hunter waited in the arena for his enraged foe to charge. He met the force of the charge with his spear which went right through its body. If the animal missed his spear-point, the hunter risked being torn to pieces, as he wore a tunic without any armour. This was just one kind of *venatio*, or beast hunt. Other hunters used bow and arrows, while some tackled bulls with their bare hands. Few hunters became as famous as champion gladiators, but the Roman poet Martial speaks of one called Carpophorus, who killed twenty beasts in a single hunt.

HERON-HAWKING. You would be surprised if *falconry* were taught at your school, yet in the Middle Ages every young nobleman had to learn how to train hawks. Training these birds took a long time and great skill. King John of England, who reigned from 1199 to 1216, passed a law allowing any free man to hawk on his own land. After this each class of person had its own special kind of hawk. Juliana Bernes, a noblewoman writing in 1486, tells us that a prince used a falcon, a priest had the sparrowhawk, while the servant used a kestrel. Herons were the special prey of the falcon, which soared on high until the dogs had *flushed* the heron from its cover.

COCK-FIGHTING AT SCHOOL. Any modern school which tried to encourage cock-fighting would soon be in deep trouble, but in the Middle Ages schoolboys often took their "cocks of the game" to school on Shrove Tuesday. The fights took place in the schoolhouse and the master received a fee for staging them. This payment was called the *cockpenny*. Grown-ups loved cock-fighting too, and every market or fair held its *main*. Cock-fighting was specially popular with army officers and naval captains, and Henry VIII built his own cock-pit in his palace.

DOGS AGAINST BEAR. You might think that the tethered bear had little chance, but most often the bear suffered wounds, while some of the dogs were killed. Robert Laneham, the English writer, tells us that if the dogs got a good hold on the bear "he would work and wind himself from them, with biting, with clawing, with roaring, with tossing and tumbling." Bear-gardens were specially built for this entertainment, but it was very popular at markets and fairs too. The man with the stick is the bear-warden who looked after the bear and tended its wounds. One famous bear, called Old Nell, used to go to an ale-house with her warden and refresh herself with beer.

STAG-HUNTING.   Cutting the throat of a stag was one way of finishing it off and Princess Elizabeth, later Elizabeth I, was happy to do so. Hunting was her favourite sport and even in old age she hunted stags every other day. Today, huntsmen often get in the news for damaging farmland and crops, but it was much worse in Elizabeth's time. William Harrison, writing in 1577, complained, "Is he a Christian that thriveth to the hurt of his neighbour in treading and breaking down his hedges, in casting open gates, in trampling of his corn, and other wise annoying him, as hunters do." At this time too, a new weapon, the gun, was becoming popular for hunting. James I of England, thought the use of guns was unfair and called it "thievish."

DANGEROUS HUNTING. A boar-hunter needed more courage than other hunters in the forests of England. He faced his quarry on foot, armed with a long boar-spear. The cross-piece below the head stopped the blade from going in too far, and the hunter held the animal at arm's length till it was killed. If something went wrong with this method, the hunter risked serious injury or death from this savage beast. As the English writer George Turberville tells us, "the boar is the only beast which can dispatch a hound at one blow." He goes on to say that he saw a boar turn on a pack of fifty hounds, and only twelve survived to get back to their kennels.

SPORT OF KINGS. Building a private race-course may seem an extravagent thing to do, yet Charles II of England, who reigned from 1660 to 1685, did just that. His race-meetings on the course near Windsor Castle were colourful, merry affairs. Charles loved to mix with his people and chat to the jockeys after the race. He also gambled on the races for very high stakes. Courses like this one were known as "bell-courses" because silver bells were given to the winners. English race-horses were highly prized abroad by this time. James I had the first Arabian stallion brought here, and bred fine horses from it. Samuel Pepys, the famous diarist, loved racing too. In his diary he complains, "This day there is a great throng to Banstead Downs upon a great horse-race. I am sorry I could not go thither."

BEAR-HUNTING. In the forests of Germany, where bears roamed in large numbers, this sport was popular with noblemen and knights. Driving the bears from their cover, the knights met them in hand-to-hand combat, using a dagger. You can see from the picture opposite why they needed to wear full armour. Other huntsmen used a bear-spear which had to be larger and stronger than other hunting spears. The blades of these weapons were sometimes two feet long. By the seventeenth century, guns were used for most bear-hunting. The wealthy hunters waited at a comfortable spot while their servants drove the bears within shooting range.

FINALLY BANNED. You can see by the looks on the faces of these men that they are enjoying the suffering of both animals. This is why the Puritans put a stop to bear-hunting during the time of the Commonwealth (1649–1660). As Thomas Macaulay, the English historian, remarks, "The Puritans hated bear-hunting, not because it gave pain to the bear, but because it gave pleasure to the spectators." During the *Restoration* it quickly became popular again, but there were always some people who wanted to ban bear-baiting because of its cruelty to the animals. More and more people came to feel this way, but they had to wait until 1835 before the British Parliament finally abolished the sport by law.

THE COCK-PIT. What a terrible place the cock-pit must have been! This picture by William Hogarth brings to life an account by Stubbes, an English writer who tells us that men flocked to the cock-pit "thick and threefold, where they gambled, swore, drank and fought amongst themselves to their hearts content." Breeders of fighting cocks spent a lot of time and money preparing their birds and put them on special diets of sugar candy and butter. During a battle the cocks wore silver spurs to improve the wounding power of their blows, and the battle went on until one of the cocks was dead or unable to fight any more. Cock-fighting went on long after bear-baiting had been banned. In 1849 Parliament made public cock-pits illegal, but private mains continued for many years afterwards.

SPANISH BULLFIGHTING. Bulls used in the *corrida* are a savage breed and were known in Roman times. Suetonius writes of, "*Iberians* who use their skins or cloaks to avoid the repeated attacks of their savage bulls before killing them." Matadors use their capes in the same way today, getting as near to the bull's horns as they dare. The mounted bullfighters

are called picadors. When the bull charges they stick their spiked poles into its neck. The banderillero has to throw darts into the bull's neck and back. All this weakens the bull and the matador kills it by thrusting a sword into its neck. The matador has the most dangerous job and many are badly injured or lose their lives.

RATTING. Of all the cruel sports we have discussed in this chapter, rat-killing is perhaps the most disgusting. It is hard to imagine anyone getting entertainment from it, yet the crowd show every sign of noisy enjoyment. Ratting was another excuse for gambling and a number of men are placing bets at the sides of the pit. The dog in this picture, called Billy, was famous for his ratting and killed a hundred rats at this meeting. Parliament banned rat-killing along with other forms of animal-baiting, but it continued at private pits till the end of the nineteenth century.

BLOODING THE FOX. Bloodsport or way of keeping down a pest? Many people argue against fox-hunting and say that it is cruel, but it does not seem to be dying out. Most counties of England have at least one hunt, like the famous Quorn hunt in Leicestershire. Hugo Meynell, the "father of modern fox-hunting," started the Quorn hunt in the eighteenth century, and fox-hunting has changed little since then. Meynell speeded up hunting by galloping after the hounds, jumping ditches and fences. During the night when the fox is away from its *earth*, a man goes out stopping up all the ways into the earth. The fox hides in a *covert* and here the hounds look for it and pick up the scent. Once the hounds have a fox's scent, the chase is on.

THREE-DAY EVENT. Show-jumping at the Olympic Games is just the third part of a three-day test of horse and rider. On the first day there is a test of training and obedience called dressage. This peaceful competition is followed by cross-country riding on the second day. Here strength and endurance matter the most. Cross-country riding is also part of the modern *pentathlon*, which includes swimming, running, fencing and pistol-shooting. The jump-off in the stadium is very exciting, with the riders competing against each other and the clock.

A DANGEROUS RACE. The sight of horses and riders crashing to the ground is very common at the Grand National. We would be surprised if no horses fell at the most difficult jumps in steeplechasing. The race was first run in 1839 at the Aintree course and is over four and a half miles, a gruelling distance with thirty jumps. A Grand National seldom goes by without a horse being killed or crippled, and many riders suffer injuries too. But if the risks are great, so is the prize-money, and the winner is famous all over the world.

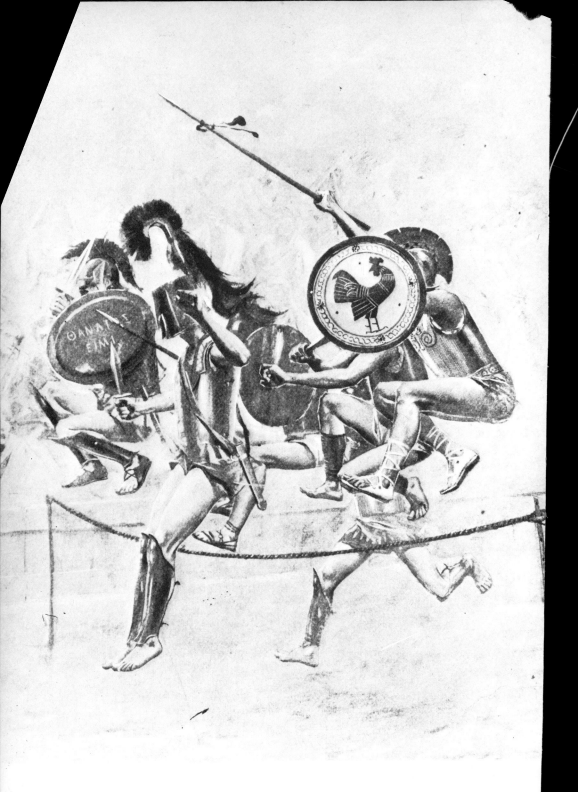

3. Skill, Strength and Stamina

When you run or jump at your school sports day, you are taking part in a kind of sport that began thousands of years ago in Greece. Greek warriors liked athletics for the same reasons we do: it kept them fit and they had the chance to test their strength against their friends and opponents.

Only the crowd in the stadium knew anything about the old Greek Olympics. The winners took days or weeks to get home and news of their victories travelled very slowly. How different it is for us! In 1972 millions of people all over the world watched the Munich Olympics on television as they happened.

For nearly two thousand years after the Greek Olympics died out, no-one organized athletic sports. There were races on village greens and stone-throwing at fairs, but not much besides. The athletics we know today started almost by accident at a few schools and universities in the middle of the last century. Within fifty years the modern Olympic Games was founded.

Baron Pierre de Coubertin, the man who started the modern Olympics, thought that taking part in the games was more important than winning. Not many people would agree with him now, and most countries spend great sums of money training their athletes. George Orwell, the great English writer, did not like big sporting events in which many countries took part. He called them "war minus the shooting." What do you think?

ANCIENT GREEK OLYMPICS. There was seldom peace between the warlike states of Greece, which did not unite until the reign of Alexander the Great in 336 B.C. However, every few years all states stopped fighting for one month while they held their Olympic festival. Athletes, wrestlers and warriors from every corner of the land gathered at the temple of Zeus near Olympia. They held this festival for the first time in 776 B.C. and it lasted for seven days. The first day was a kind of opening ceremony when the athletes gave sacrifices to Zeus. Then there were five days of sport. On the last day the winners, like the one pictured opposite, marched to the temple of Zeus and thanked the god for their victory. The games ended with a banquet.

JUMPS AND THROWS. Three of our modern "field events" were part of the ancient pentathlon: long jump, discus and javelin. The Greek long-jumper had to jump with a lead weight in each hand. You might think these weights would hold him back, but they were meant to balance his flight through the air. Phayllus, a famous Greek athlete, managed to jump eighteen feet while carrying these weights. Greek discus throwing was much more like our modern sport, but the thrower did not spin round like today's athletes. A servant put a peg in the ground where the bronze discus fell, and measured to a straight line in front of the thrower.

RACES ON FOOT. As they stood waiting for the signal at the start of a race, Greek runners faced a straight track about 180 metres long. They ran all their races, even long distances, over this straight course, turning sharply at each end. This kind of running was another part of the pentathlon. For warriors there was a special race run in full armour. They had to carry their shields and weapons too, and jump over rope hurdles (as in the picture on page 50). Winners of Olympic events were great heroes in their home towns. The Greek writer Plato says that Athens awarded "free meals at the town hall" to each Athenian who won at the Olympic Games.

THROWING AND CASTING. Early English athletics was very rough and ready compared with the Greek games. The poor people of London liked throwing heavy stones, bars of iron or logs of wood. They did too much of this for Edward III, who reigned from 1327 to 1377. Edward was worried because people were not practising enough archery, so he banned these sports. Noblemen thought such pastimes were beneath them, but changed their minds later, when none other than King Henry VIII took up weight-throwing.

ROYAL HAMMER-THROW. Can you imagine this
hammer being used in today's Olympic field event?
It is just an ordinary blacksmith's sledge hammer with
a stiff wooden handle. Throwing this kind of hammer
began in Britain in the twelfth century and became a
popular sport at fairs held in churchyards. Here the
thrower is Henry VIII, who reigned from 1509 to
1547. He was a keen sportsman and tried his hand at
most sports, though he did not seem to bother with
special clothes for his sporting activities!

GRAND SHOOTING-MATCH. From military practice to healthy pastime—that is the story of archery. Henry VIII was a fine archer and made every man in his kingdom train to shoot with the long bow, as this made for a strong army in wartime. There were three kinds of target called rover, prick and butt. The target in this picture is a prick, made of canvas with a wooden peg at the centre. Once the musket had been invented, armies gradually stopped using the long bow, but archery matches remained a pleasant pastime. An English doctor called Jones advised his patients to go "shooting at garden butts; this practice of all others the manliest leaves no part of the body unexercised."

HIGHLAND GAMES. The shot-putt is our modern version of this event from the Highland Games in Scotland. These games took place at the meetings of Scottish clans and were not a sporting event by themselves. Scottish clans held meetings to do business and plan battles, and the clansmen passed the time testing each other's strength at different sports, such as running, jumping, hammer-throwing and tossing the *caber*. After 1745 the clans no longer held meetings, so the games stopped, but people started them again in the nineteenth century, mostly for fun at holiday time.

COLLEGE FOOT-GRIND. Today we would laugh at anyone turning out in cricket boots and flannels to run a steeplechase. But this kind of athletics began as a pastime for young men at university, and proper running gear was unknown. All the same, they did take their running seriously and began to train for meetings. The races brought large crowds of spectators and ordinary people wanted to take part. Up and down the country men formed athletics clubs, and held their own race-meetings. In 1880, twenty seven of these clubs formed the Amateur Athletic Association, the famous three A's, which still governs athletics in this country today.

SIX DAY WALK. This may not be our idea of athletics, but it was just what Victorian crowds wanted to see. There was a good chance of seeing a walker collapse, and people gambled on the endurance of the contestants. Such a race was more like our non-stop roller-skating than real athletics. Men often walked on the open road, like Foster Powell, who hit the headlines by walking from London to York and back in six days. Walking races over set distances gradually became part of proper athletics meetings. Today there are two walking races in the Olympic games: the twenty thousand and the fifty thousand metres.

GYMNASTIC FETE. There are one or two things here which we would not call gymnastics today. Can you spot them? In the nineteenth century gymnastics was just beginning to be a sport, and this picture looks more like a garden party than a serious athletics meeting. One piece of equipment here is still used

in modern Olympic gymnastics—the parallel bars in the right hand corner. Many sporting events took place in the building and grounds of the Crystal Palace, which was built for the Great Exhibition of 1851.

SPORTS DAY. Try and judge the height of the bar in this pole-vault event. It is probably less than half the present world record! In Victorian times, pole-vaulting, like many other kinds of athletic events, was just beginning. The first kind of pole-vaulting was called broad-jumping and tested how far, not how high, a man could leap using a pole. Even from a height of eight or nine feet the falling pole-vaulter could hurt himself quite badly. It is surprising that there is nothing to protect him on the ground beneath the bar.

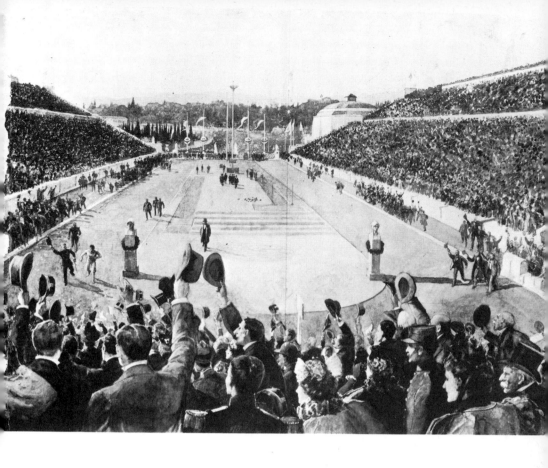

THE MARATHON. In 490 B.C. the Greek army defeated the Persian invaders at the battle of Marathon. A great runner, called Pheidippides, ran from Marathon to Athens to bring news of the victory, and then died. At the first modern Olympics held at Athens in 1896, long distance runners from all over the world had come to run in the footsteps of Pheidippides, a distance of more than twenty six miles. What a surprise for the Greek crowd when Spiridon Loues, an unknown Greek shepherd, entered the stadium first! The crowd went wild, as you can see above, and two Greek princes escorted their hero to the winning post.

HELPED OVER THE LINE. Following the excitement of Athens, the next two Olympics were dull
affairs. At Paris and St. Louis, the games were little
more than side-shows to trade fairs. But there was
plenty to argue about at the London games in 1908,
and again the Marathon event turned out to be the
most surprising race. This picture shows the little
Italian, Dorando, running through the streets of
London on his way to the stadium. He got there first,
but was so exhausted that he collapsed on the track.
Some track officials helped him up, but his legs gave
way again, and his helpers half-carried him over the
line. Sadly, Dorando was disqualified for this, and the
race went to Hayes of the U.S.A., who crossed the
line second, but without any help.

THE TORCH BEARER. The Second World War had put a stop to two Olympic Games. In 1948 London was the site of the first Olympics since those at Berlin in 1936. The custom of bringing the Olympic flame from Greece, started at the Berlin Olympics, continued, and here the last runner is arriving at Wembley Stadium. Behind the runner are the famous words of Baron de Coubertin, the founder of the modern Olympics. The great star of these games was a woman called Fannie Blankers-Koen, from the Netherlands. She surprised everyone by winning four gold medals in the sprints and hurdles.

JAVELIN THROWING. We have seen that some kind of shot-putt and hammer-throw has been practised for centuries. But after the ancient Olympic Games no-one threw javelins for sport, only in warfare. Javelin throwing was not even revived at the first modern Olympics, but had to wait until 1912. Since then athletes have made great improvements, adding over one hundred feet to the world record. As it is the only throwing event which allows a run-up, there are strict rules about how the javelin must be thrown. Some Spanish athletes tried throwing the javelin by turning round and round like hammer throwers. This method produced very long throws, but was banned because it was too dangerous. No-one could tell where the javelin would land!

HAMMER THROWING. It is hardly surprising that this athlete can throw his hammer much further than Henry VIII could. The shape and balance of the modern hammer is designed to help the athlete's throw. In his seven-foot circle the thrower turns, building up speed from the back of the circle. At the end of his third turn he releases the hammer. Emigrants from Britain took hammer-throwing to America, and there they greatly improved the distance thrown. The present world record is now more than three times the first recorded distance, thrown at a meeting in 1866.

POLE-VAULTING. This athlete may look as if he is falling back, put in fact he is well on his way to clearing the very high bar. Athletes had made remarkable improvements in pole-vaulting, helped by the invention of the fibreglass pole. As you can see, this kind of pole bends, and when it straightens out it whips the vaulter over the bar. Compared with the old wooden pole-vaulting we saw earlier, fibreglass vaulting is a very scientific event. It attracts some of the strongest, most skillful and bravest athletes in the world.

THE TRAGIC GAMES. The Olympic Games is an occasion when we all hope that nations will forget their enemies and live for sport, as the ancient Greeks did. The games at Munich in 1972 promised to be the biggest and best so far. Here you can see the colourful opening ceremony which took place in the magnificent stadium built by the Germans. But when Arab terrorists murdered some Israeli athletes, the games were ruined. The sporting events went on, but no-one could forget the tragedy. Perhaps future Olympics will have to be much smaller and more easily controlled. They may even be replaced by separate world championships in each different sport.

4. Ball-games

Most of you will have played a game of football with an old tennis ball, and enjoyed doing so, even though you were using the "wrong" ball. The idea of using special balls for different games is not very old. The Romans certainly used different kinds of ball, some hard and small, others large and light. But they played their games with the kind of ball they liked or happened to have.

In early times few ball-games had proper rules. Hand-ball games were played with the hand, sometimes with "gloves," or with hand-held bats, clubs and rackets. Foot-ball games allowed kicking the ball. Hand-ball games developed into separate games like tennis, cricket and stoolball while football was still a mad scramble, more like all-in wrestling.

Soccer may have been a late starter, but it made up for that by quickly becoming the most popular sport in England. Unlike athletes, soccer stars are professionals and can earn large sums of money. This has made soccer into a big business all over the world, for it is popular in more countries than any other ball-game.

The other ball-games in this chapter have become international too. Tennis and golf are among the most popular and offer big prize money to professional players. Only a few countries play cricket seriously, but those which do show no signs of letting it die out. We have not yet seen a Test match on television live from Australia, but no doubt we soon will.

GREEK BALL-GAMES. We do not know anything
about the rules of the game in the picture above, or if
there were "goals," but it certainly looks like a form of
hockey. From very early times the Greeks played ball-
games. Homer tells us that the lovely princess
Nausicaa played at ball with her maids. When she
threw the ball into a river by mistake, her maids cried
out and woke up Odysseus, the great hero of the
Trojan war.

LAZY HAND-BALL. Roman ball-games could be
hard work, but not this one! The players are using a
ball called a *follis*, which was soft and filled with air,
and most popular with older men and women.
Petronius, the Roman comic writer, tells us about "a
bald old man in a reddish shirt playing at ball with
some long-haired boys . . . The old gentleman never
picked up the ball if it touched the ground. A slave
stood by with a bagful and supplied them to the
players." Another Roman called Spurinna carried on
playing hand-ball till he was seventy-seven. The
Romans played their ball-games on the Campus
Martius, a large open space in the city, like our common
or park.

CLUB-BALL. This game was an early form of cricket played in the Middle Ages, and the club was usually straight. The man on the right is using a stick that looks like a stump with a point for sticking in the ground. The club was also a handy weapon when players lost their tempers. During a quarrel over a game in 1420, one player hit another with his club, breaking his head and shoulder. The wounded man lay paralysed for three months, unable to hear or see.

STREET "HOCKEY." If this early form of hockey had any rules, we do not know much about them. Probably a player had to run from one end of the street to the other without losing the wooden ball, while the rest tried to get it from him. At Leicester, on Shrove Tuesday, men and boys played hockey in the castle grounds. Other men, called Whipping Toms, chased the hockey players and lashed them with whips. The Whipping Toms could not strike above the knees, so the hockey players could kneel down for safety.

MEDIEVAL FOOTBALL. These children are having a harmless kick-about, but most football "matches" at this time were more risky affairs. In cities men played their football games in the street. In the country neighbouring villages played a "match" over a space of two or three miles, each side trying to get the ball back to their own village. Play was very rough and sometimes men were killed. In 1322 a priest, called William de Spalding, was wearing an unsheathed knife while playing football. In one tackle for the ball, he killed a friend by accident. Football remained a rough and dangerous game for centuries. Sir Thomas Elyot, writing in 1531, says "football is nothing but beastly fury and extreme violence, whereof procedeth hurt."

LOOK, NO RACKETS! You will all know how much fun there is in hitting, throwing and catching a ball with your friends. Ordinary people of England in the Middle Ages thought so too. Hand-ball was a game they could afford. They could make a ball from cloth or leather stuffed with hair, and needed no special court for their game. We know nothing about the rules of their hand-ball games. Most likely the players tried to keep the ball in the air as long as possible. Some players began to wear "gloves" to hit the ball harder. We can assume that rackets developed from these "gloves," and this is how the first sort of tennis began.

COURT TENNIS. A piece of rope tied to a pillar at
one end and held by a player at the other was the
only "net" that was needed for a tennis match in the
seventeenth century. No doubt the players took turns
at the boring job of holding the rope. But there were
specially built tennis courts too, with a place for
spectators. Here the rope had tassels hanging down
to make something more like our net. Charles II of
England was a keen tennis player and liked to be
applauded whether he deserved it or not. Pepys wrote
in 1664, "I went to the tennis court, and there saw
the King play at tennis, but to see how the King's play
is extolled, without any cause at all, was a loathsome
sight."

A "ROUGH" GAME. By modern standards the ground where these men are playing is hardly a "golf course," but that did not stop golf from being popular. The game we know today had its birth-place in Scotland. In the fifteenth century men were so keen to play golf that they did not practise their archery. As the bow and arrow were still the main weapons of warfare, rulers were against anything which stopped men practising their skill. James II of Scotland, who reigned from 1437 to 1460, tried to ban golf by law, but it did not work. By the seventeenth century golf had spread to England, where a club was formed at Blackheath in 1608.

TWO-STUMP CRICKET. The cricket match being played in this picture had a proper set of rules. But some of the things will surprise you—the number of stumps, the shape of the bat, and the way of bowling. London and South East England was the home of cricket at this time. In 1729 the "Evening Post" reported that a London team played "the Dartford men for a considerable sum of money, wagers and bets, and the latter beat the former very much." Spectators at these games supported their side noisily and sometimes with violence, and many gambled heavily on the result.

RUGBY FOOTBALL BEGINS. Imagine up to three hundred boys kicking and chasing one ball, pushing and tackling each other and dodging among trees, all for two hours or so! The boys could catch the ball to get a better kick at it, but they could not run forward with it. This was what football at Rugby school was like, until a boy called William Webb Ellis tried something different. At a match in 1823 he caught the ball and sprinted forward with it. His opponents said he was cheating, but the idea of running with the ball became popular. Soon other schools with large playing fields were playing this form of "Rugby."

THE DRIBBLING GAME. Some schools had very small playing fields, or just yards surrounded by buildings. They could not play "Rugby," so they developed dribbling to keep the ball low. The boys could neither handle the ball nor kick it forward. Both the new kinds of football became popular at universities, and soon ordinary people wanted to play too. They formed "soccer" or "Rugby" clubs in their home towns. Members of the "soccer" clubs met in London in 1863 to make proper rules for their game, and formed the Football Association. In 1872 they bought a silver cup as a prize in the first F.A. cup competition. A London club called the Wanderers beat the Royal Engineers in the final.

ENGLISH CRICKET "DIES." New ways of bowling helped cricket to progress from the kind we saw in the earlier picture to that of today. Underarm bowling died out because roundarm was better for getting wickets, and roundarm gave way to overarm as the best of all. Faster bowling meant a need for protective clothing, though the batsmen here are not wearing gloves. The scene of this picture is one of the most famous cricket matches ever played, when Australia beat England in a Test match for the first time in England. The bearded English batsman is W. G. Grace, "the champion" cricketer of the nineteenth century. Even his great batting was helpless against the Australian bowler Spofforth, known as "the demon." Australia won the match by seven runs and one spectator dropped down dead with excitement. This notice appeared in a newspaper the next day: "In affectionate remembrance of English cricket, which died at the Oval on the 29th August, 1882."

LAWN TENNIS. Where are the stands, the royal box, the linesmen, the ball-boys and all the other things we see at Wimbledon today? They were added later in Wimbledon's history, for at the time of the picture, in 1881, lawn tennis had just been invented. In 1873 a retired army Major, called Wingfield, invented a form of lawn tennis to be played on a court shaped like an hour-glass! People liked his game but found some of the rules difficult to follow. Funny though it may seem, the Marylebone Cricket Club was asked to correct the faults in Major Wingfield's new game. Not surprisingly their new rules were little better. When the first lawn tennis tournament took place at Wimbledon in 1877, a different set of rules were drawn up, and these have lasted to the present day.

RUGBY FOOTBALL TODAY. A scrummage can be a dangerous place to be, and most Rugby players are well-built and tough. There are now two kinds of Rugby played in Britain. The game shown here is Rugby Union, and its players are strictly amateurs. An argument about money caused some members of the Union to break away and start a game of their own. They wanted players to be paid, at first for loss of earnings and later as professional players. These clubs, mostly in Lancashire and Yorkshire, formed the Rugby League. The Rugby League altered the rules of the Union game, and their sides have thirteen players, two less than Rugby Union teams.

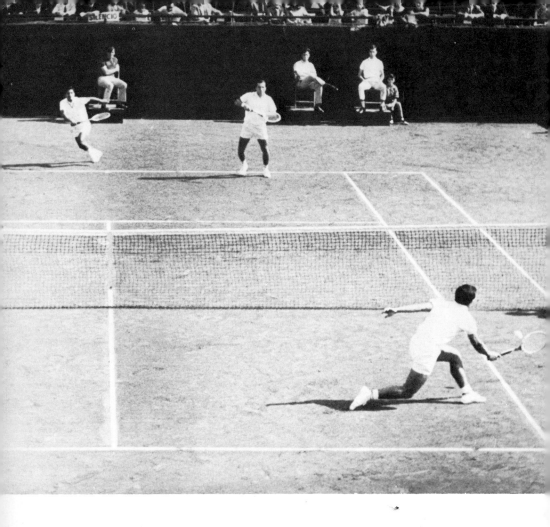

INTERNATIONAL TENNIS. Wimbledon has been an "open" tournament since 1968, and amateurs and professionals can play together, but they are playing for themselves. In the Davis cup matches players represent their countries in a world championship for nations. The first Davis cup contest was played in 1900, and was named after the man who donated the cup. The United States won then and has won many times since. Five matches have to be played in a Davis cup contest, four singles and one doubles. More and more countries are taking part in Davis cup contests, as tennis becomes more popular throughout the world.

HOW'S THAT? The wicket-keeper catches the ball, the fielders appeal, the umpire raises his finger and the batsman begins his long walk back to the dressing room. Being caught is just one of nine ways of getting out, some of them very rare. Do you know the other eight? Cricket has never become a world-wide sport and only seven countries play Test matches. Yet in those seven countries people play and watch cricket with great enthusiasm. In England county clubs have begun to play "limited over" games, designed to make both batting and bowling more exciting. People who are not interested in the finer points of cricket can enjoy these quick-scoring prize-matches.

WATCHING AND PLAYING.   Perhaps you support one of the "super" teams like Arsenal or Liverpool, even though these clubs are many miles from where you live. You can do this because you know there is a good chance of frequently seeing these teams on television. But there are many clubs who do not have much support and spend most of their time trying to keep out of debt. Very few teams can expect big crowds whenever they play, and falling attendances worry people who care about football. Away from the professional scene, ordinary people still love playing football. School soccer is very popular, while almost every village and town has its local side playing in hundreds of leagues throughout the country.

Table of Dates

776 B.C.	First Greek Olympic Games.
490 B.C.	Pheidippides runs the first Marathon.
80 A.D.	Opening of the Colosseum at Rome.
1540	Henry VIII founds "The Maisters of the Noble Science of Defence."
1640	First race-meeting held at Newmarket.
1787	Formation of the Marylebone Cricket Club.
1823	Webb Ellis runs with the ball at Rugby.
1835	British Parliament bans the baiting of animals.
1863	Formation of the Football Association.
1865	Marquess of Queensbury drew up rules for boxing.
1871	Formation of the Rugby Football Union.
1877	First lawn tennis tournament at Wimbledon.
	First ever Test match, between England and Australia, held at Melbourne.
1880	Formation of the Amateur Athletic Association.
1896	First modern Olympics, held at Athens.
1898	Formation of the Amateur Fencing Association.
1930	First World Cup soccer competition, won by Uruguay.
1966	World Cup competition held in, and won by, England.
1968	First "Open" Wimbledon tennis tournament.
1972	Olympic Games held at Munich in West Germany.

New Words

Amphitheatre	A large Roman arena where games were held.
Caber	A large log of wood tossed at the Highland Games in Scotland.
Caesar	A Roman family name, later used to mean emperor.
Caesti	Roman boxing-gloves made of leather studded with iron pellets.
Cockpenny	A Medieval schoolmaster's fee for staging cockfights.
Corrida	A Spanish bullfight.
Covert	Bushes or trees where a fox is hiding.
Earth	The underground home of a fox.
Essedarii	Roman gladiators who fought from chariots.
Factions	Four different teams in a Roman chariot race.
Falconry	The art of training birds of prey to hunt for man.
Flush	To use dogs to chase prey from its hiding place.
Foils	Blunt-edged swords with points shielded by buttons.
Follis	A large soft ball filled with air, used by the Romans.
Iberians	People from Spain and Portugal.
Libitinarii	Roman slaves who carried dead gladiators from the arena.

Main	The name for a group of cock-fights at the pit.
Matadors	Spanish bullfighters who kill the bull.
Metae	Turning-posts at the ends of a Roman race track.
Mufflers	An early form of boxing glove used in eighteenth century England.
Naumachia	A "mock" sea battle held in a flooded Roman arena.
Pentathlon	A five part event in the Greek Olympics: long jump, discus, javelin, running and wrestling.
Podium	The lowest terrace of a Roman arena, with the best seats.
Quintain	A target used in tilting practice.
Restoration	The time after the Commonwealth when Charles II was king.
Retiarius	A Roman gladiator armed with a net and a trident.
Secutor	A Roman gladiator armed with a sword and a shield.
Venabulum	A large Roman spear with an iron point, used in beast-hunts.
Venatio	A Roman beast-hunt in the arena.

More Books

Auguet R. *Cruelty and Civilisation: The Roman Games* (Allen and Unwin, 1972). A detailed account for older readers of all the events in the Roman arena, with some excellent pictures.

Johnston B. *All about Cricket* (W. H. Allen, 1972). History of cricket, great Test matches, famous players, records and hints on play. All told interestingly by a famous cricket commentator.

McNab T. *Athletics—Field Events* (Brockhampton Press, 1972). An illustrated Teach Yourself book, with notes on the history, techniques and standards of all field events. There is a companion book called *Athletics—Track Events.*

Revie A. *Wonderful Wimbledon* (Pelham Books, 1972). The story of lawn tennis at Wimbledon from its beginning to the present day.

Sutherland E. and K. *Complete book of Sport* (Ward Lock, 1969). Brief history, rules and techniques of thirty-five sports from archery to wrestling, with good pictures and diagrams.

Wymer N. *Sport in England* (Harrap, 1949). Though a little out of date on modern sport, this book is excellent for information about sports in the past, with good pictures.

Young P. M. *A History of British Football* (Stanley Paul, 1968). A lengthy account of football from ancient times, full of interesting detail for older readers.